If you are looking for something practical, a book with handles, this is the tool you need to begin the open conversation with your son.

Scott Chevalier
Pastor and Speaker
Founder of Powerhouse Youth Project

Eric has a powerful yet simple way of explaining deep truths with practical application. I wholeheartedly recommend this book to every dad.

David Ask
Recording Artist and Author

I wish my dad would have had this book when I was growing up! This book has given me the shot of courage I needed to begin this vital conversation with my boys.

Aubrey McGowan
Founder of Family Field Guide

With this guide, Eric Poulin, delivers the simple words, honest answers, and easy analogies every dad needs to teach his sons about sex. The world is dangerous and the stakes are too high to ignore our job by leaving our kids to figure it out on their own. You can do it and this tool will help!

Seth Buechley
Author, Ambition: Leading with Gratitude
CEO of Cathedral Consulting

JUST KEEP IT IN YOUR PANTS?

HOW WISE DADS TALK TO THEIR SONS ABOUT SEX, LOVE AND PORNOGRAPHY

ERIC POULIN

Paperback: 978-1-64184-049-1

Ebook: 978-1-64184-050-7

Dedication

To Anna, Thank you for your unwavering love. Thank you for always being in my corner and cheering me on. Thank you for giving me four beautiful boys and thank you for nurturing them so well. I love you and I always will.

To Caden, Asher, Jayce and Ari. I am so proud to be your father and so proud of who you are. I love how you are growing in the Lord and how you love and protect each other. Even when you are pounding on your brothers, I know you love them. We will continue to learning together how to use our strength to fight for beauty in all things. I am grateful to the Father for allowing me to be your Dad. There is no greater pleasure as your dad, then watching you grow and it is my great privilege to shepherd you. Keep your eyes on Him, the author and perfecter of your faith who for the joy set before Him endured the cross, despising the shame, sat down at the right hand of the throne of God...For you. I love you boys.

Contents

Forward

The song, "ABC" is a 1970 #1 hit by The Jackson 5. It was released on February 24, 1970.

What a simple song title for the Jackson 5. The title of Eric Poulin's book is simple, yet at the same time very profound. "Just Keep it in Your Pants?" covers a sticky subject in a very practical way and gives you, the reader, a very hands on approach to communicating to your boys about three simple letters, "SEX" and the need for a healthy opportunity for all dad's or caregivers to communicate with the boys in their sphere of influence.

As a former youth pastor, and lead pastor, I can tell you how needed this "open approach" process, that Eric describes in his own home, is needed in the homes across our nation. It breaks down the barriers and eliminates the "dirty" in sex and the fear that most fathers experience when thinking about the "talk". I think that has been the issue in most of our homes. We often refer to this discussion as a moment in time, as if it has been scheduled in our day planners and we await our alarm to begin the discussion. No wonder we all sit in fear waiting for the right time and secretly hoping for someone else to deliver the message to our sons.

In Genesis 3, God comes looking for Adam and asks, "Where are you?" I don't believe an all-knowing, always present God had a GPS issue with Adam. God was not asking for Adam's physical, geographic location, rather it was a question of "position". God had placed Adam first in the garden and rather than accept his position, Adam surrendered his position and in doing so released his responsibility for the family. God is looking for men today to assume their position and accept the responsibility to lead in our homes. "Just Keep it in Your Pants?" is a call to every man to step up and assume their position as leader.

I have known Eric for more than 30 years and I have seen him shake off the broken examples that failed to lead for him, and seek out new models of men and dad's in order to be at his best for his own boys one day. That one day has arrived, and his example and answer to the call in this book provides such a solid model for men of all ages. If you did not have a healthy model as a father, this is a must read for you to redefine sexuality for your future sons and redefine for you a healthy view of sex in marriage. If you are looking for something practical, a book with handles, this is the tool you need to begin the open conversation with your son(s).

Thank you Eric, for asking me to write this forward and I most certainly will have a copy for my own son to read and prepare himself for this journey. Your example in front of the Poulin boys is all that is right with families and you have made SEX as easy as ABC.

Scott Chevalier

Introduction

There are so many stories about how a boy becomes a man, and so many of them are right on track. They tell of the eternal heroic heart woven into all men. They tell of the eternal quest that courses through our very veins and even calls us to go deeper into a story we cannot see. These epic tales of hero, lover, leader and father are beautiful, but they make us ache inside as well because we know something is missing and left unfinished in each of us. These stories, whether true or fiction, ring so true in us that we keep coming back to relive these moments in movies, books, songs, poetry and even listening to our fathers and grandfathers tell the same stirring stories over and over again.

I don't know about you, but when I was a boy, I dreamed of being the hero more days than not. I longed to slay the "bad guy" who walked into our classroom, meaning to do harm, and then be the humble hero who knocked him out with one punch. I didn't care one bit what the other boys would think, but I couldn't stop replaying in my mind what all the girls would say and do after I became that hero. I would rehearse these moments in my mind over and over to the point I could feel my heart beating in my chest. At the time it seemed so normal and automatic to think these thoughts, and normal, it was. In fact, it was God-breathed. My heart and the heart of all men long to be this hero. Why? We are made in the image of God and His son Jesus Christ – the true Hero. Period.

God made the hero in each of us tied very closely to our sexuality. Our desire to "slay dragons" has nothing to do with violence or conquering for the sake of conquering. We were made with a mission and that mission is to drive out darkness and to protect what is beautiful. Our sexual drive is aimed right at the most beautiful thing in the world, "Her." There is no question that "She" is the most captivating beauty on earth. Kings of the earth will sacrifice their entire kingdoms for this beauty. So, why are things such a mess in this area for most men? We have a problem… that problem is called sin. Sin has ruined everything. It has blinded us, it has stolen our voices and made it almost impossible to hear and act in Truth. At the same time this "sin" is not a surprise to God. In His sovereign goodness, and so that we would know his character as Redeemer, Comforter, Keeper and Healer, we have entered into a dangerous world. But we are not alone. It is His plan that we lead our sons and others around us into truth and light and especially in the areas that are most sensitive to our natures. Our sexuality is good, intense and quite often misguided.

Eric Poulin has written a practical and inspiring book that explains how we can very quickly and carefully lead our sons well in the area of sexuality.

Most of our problems with sexuality are purely from a lack of leadership by our own fathers. I love how Eric weaves God's truth into each topic and then simply explains how to skillfully navigate these conversations with our sons. He explains that at every age there are appropriate topics and he gives us ways to make these conversations less awkward. So, get out your pen and highlighter and dive in!

David Ask

1

Giving The Talk

"Children are a heritage from the Lord, offspring a reward from him. Like arrows in the hands of a warrior are children born in one's youth." Psalm 127:3–4

Raising my four boys has been the most fun, adventurous, and sometimes challenging responsibility of my life. I love being a dad. I love seeing the world through the eyes of my boys. I love watching them learn new things. I love how they mispronounce words. I love that I get to teach them how to throw a ball. How to cast a fishing pole. How to cook eggs. I love that each day I get to try again to point them to Jesus.

But I don't particularly love some of the tougher responsibilities of being a father. And sometimes I find myself "checking out" rather than leading them either by example or through intentional direction.

As a young man, I often thought about being a dad, and I had a lot of great ideas about how I was going to parent. I didn't know my father growing up, which I'm sure contributed to those dreams of not only being a dad but being one that was fully invested in raising my kids. I wasn't on my own entirely, though, because I was fortunate to have had mentors and a step-father in my life who helped shape me into who I am today.

When I was a young man thinking about my future family, it was natural to think of all the fun things I would do with my kids. But there was one thing I hadn't thought of, which is quite a challenge—addressing the subject of sex once my boys were old enough to begin having those conversations. Who thinks of that?

When my oldest was about five or six years old, I figured I still had plenty of time. I thought I would sit down with him in four or five years and lay it all out. You know, the "birds and the bees" talk? Then I would be prepared. Until that time came and everything I had rehearsed went right out the window. I had no idea how to begin.

Do you remember when your parents gave you "the talk"? Or maybe they never discussed it with you. But if they did, it probably went something like this:

You and your dad are riding down the road, walking through a park or maybe sitting in the living room.

"Son, your mom wants me to talk to you about something. You . . . ahh . . . you know where babies come from, right?"

"Yeah, Dad. I'm 14. I've heard."

"Oh, good. Alright then. Well, just keep it in your pants."

My parents skimmed over it a little, but from what I recall, it was a topic that they avoided.

Do you ever feel anxious about talking to your kids about sex? Does the idea make you feel ill-equipped? Maybe you're not sure how to start the conversation. I used to feel that way too. But instead of trying to find the perfect moment to introduce my boys to anatomy, sex, and the dangers of pornography, I started with what they could understand, for the stage each one was in.

**Remember this:
Simple words, honest answers and easy analogies.**

What I found was that it wasn't hard when we just had the short conversations and short followup talks as needed. Remember this: Simple words, honest answers and easy analogies.

When a dad learns how to communicate wisely and effectively with his son, conversations about sex, money, faith and any other essential topic will begin to flow naturally. Some of these discussions will be spontaneous while others will be planned. But in each case, a dad needs to start communicating early and often so that when the time comes, he is not paralyzed when wanting to train up his son in these different areas.

Just about anyone can teach our children the basics about sex, but as parents, only we can put it in the proper context, within the safety of our homes and in a way that they can understand.

I used to think that by giving my sons the facts about sex, I would rob them of their innocence. Maybe you feel the same way, assuming you'll do more harm than good. But it hasn't been a negative experience at all. Instead, it has equipped them to understand that sex is a gift from God and a beautiful expression of love in the context of a committed marriage.

What robs children of their innocence is a lack of knowledge.

What robs children of their innocence is a lack of knowledge. The reality is that too many children learn about sex from everyone but their parents. Whether it's playground slang or a distorted description of intercourse from another child. Often, seeing pornography is what provides a child's first jarring glimpse of sex and robs them of their innocence.

In the following pages are questions I have discovered to be common among dads. I don't have all the answers, but hopefully, I can be of some help and get you thinking more about how to approach the topic with your son.

2

When And How To Begin

Listen, my son, to your father's instruction, and don't reject your mother's teaching. - Proverbs 1:8

Begin as soon as possible. Yes, ASAP! If you have a child who can talk, then you should begin now. Even if he is three. Start by teaching him the correct names for his body parts. An ear is an ear; a nose is a nose; a penis is a penis; a vagina is a vagina; a belly button is a belly button.

It's essential that we do not call their body parts by nicknames. We don't want our children to have a negative view of their body parts. If we associate a boy's penis with shame, it will be much more difficult and embarrassing for him as he gets older.

Recently I was talking with a friend, who said, "Well, what if my five-year-old says 'penis' in public?" My response was: "Then you're doing well. Teaching your son accurately about sex is nothing to be ashamed about."

I often remind my younger boys that their penis and testicles are their "private parts" and that no one is allowed to touch or see them. I also remind them that if someone does touch them in that area, they should tell me right away without ever worrying about getting in trouble.

If you have a son who is between seven and ten, he is at a pivotal season. And the way you engage, guide, and love him will shape the rest of his life—and that includes his views on sex.

If your son is ten or older and you have not had any of these types of conversations yet, I would encourage you to make this a *top priority*. Even if you homeschool and think that he hasn't heard about it from peers or media, you should consider starting the conversation soon.

Where do you begin? I'd say the first step is to begin with what he already knows. If you are not sure, ask him. You might be surprised what he already knows. Or, what he thinks he knows. I was a little surprised recently when I asked my oldest about what he thought about a particular topic that he heard about. His understanding was far from accurate but, it gave us the opportunity to get some clarity and to be informed accurately.

Next talk about the goodness of God. How He created our bodies, and how males are different from females. How we have been designed for beauty, and how we don't need to be ashamed of attraction to girls.

These first two steps don't need to be scheduled on the calendar. But they should be on your radar and be part of your parenting. When the opportunity comes up in your day to day conversations, seize the moment and use it to ask your children what they know or to remind them that they have been created by God uniquely different than girls.

This approach may seem oversimplified, but it is an excellent way to lay the foundation. Since my sons know that a boy has a penis and a girl has a vagina, it was not uncomfortable when they first asked me how our dogs got pregnant. I merely gave them an elementary lesson on mating. It wasn't an awkward discussion, and it didn't last very long, but it was another building block for future conversations.

Take Aways:

1. Talk about how our bodies are made.
2. Talk about how males and females are different.
3. Teach him the correct name for body parts.
4. Use simple words, honest answers and easy analogies.

3

Where Babies Come From

For it was You who created my inward parts; You knit me together in my mother's womb. I will praise You because I have been remarkably and wonderfully made. - Psalms 139:13

When my boys asked me where babies came from, the first answer was that God created them in their mom's belly. I told them that after nine months or so, babies are ready to come out and that many times, doctors help deliver the baby. Usually, answers like this will be enough for them.

Recently, I was putting my four-year-old to bed, and we were talking about rocket ships and fishing and the events of the day. Then he asked how babies got out of their mom's bellies. I had previously left it at "Doctor's help the mom at the hospital," but since this was a follow-up conversation that he initiated, I had a choice to make and I think I made the correct one.

I reminded him that in his private area he has a penis and that in a girl's private areas, she has a vagina. Then I told him that when it is time for the baby to come out of the mother's belly, the mom's vagina opens up and the baby comes out of a tube connected to the mother's belly.

He wasn't shocked or scared or uncomfortable. He only said, "Oh. So the tube in the ve-*china* opens, and then the doctors give the baby to the mom? Did that happen to me?"

The next morning, I asked him if he remembered how babies got from the belly to the mom's arms, and he said yes. From the "china."

No need to elaborate with more info unless your young child has additional questions. When they do come, at that point, answer with simple words in a calm voice.

Take Aways:

1. When speaking about the basics, begin by reviewing what you have already discussed.
2. Find opportunities to have short follow-up conversations.
3. Use simple words, honest answers and easy analogies.

4

Explaining Sex

God blessed them, and God said to them, "Be fruitful, multiply, fill the earth, and subdue it… - Genesis 1:28

First, sex came from God, and God gives good things to His children. When we look at Genesis, we see that Adam and Eve came together physically. God blessed them, and God said to them, "Be fruitful, multiply…" Also interpreted as, "Be fruitful and get it on…".

By the time I had the first intercourse conversation with my son, it was no longer awkward, because we had already had prior discussions. I simply told him that when a man and woman are naked together, the man will put his penis into the woman's vagina, and sometimes the woman will get pregnant. Other times she won't get pregnant. I told him that sex is good. Sex is for making babies. And sex is designed by God to help build a close bond between a husband and wife.

It seems popular today to view Christians and the Bible as essentially anti-sexual, treating sex as a kind of necessary evil. But this is not what the Bible says. God's Word teaches on the subject of sex directly and candidly.

Here is an excellent summary of what it has to say about sex, taken from Dr. William Coles's book *Sex and Love in the Bible*:

> Sex is good. It is the creation of God, and all men are expected to enjoy it. No prudishness or squeamishness is appropriate. Sex is not an occasion for shame or embarrassment. All members of a family must learn to use their sexual drives responsibly, but they do so by facing the facts openly, not by hiding behind blinders, pretending that life is asexual, that such matters are never discussed in polite society.

Secondly, sex was intended to bring a husband and wife closer together and to be enjoyed thoroughly. In Proverbs 5:18-19, Solomon tells his sons:

> "Let your fountain be blessed, and rejoice in the wife of your youth, a lovely deer, a graceful doe.

Let her breasts fill you at all times with delight; be intoxicated always in her love."

Take Aways:

1. Sex is when a man will put his penis into the woman's vagina.
2. After having sex, sometimes the woman will get pregnant.
3. Sex is designed by God to make babies and to help married couples build close bonds between each other.
4. Use simple words, honest answers and easy analogies.

5

Who Should Have Sex

Drink water from your own well, share your love only with your wife. Why spill the water of your springs in the streets, having sex with just anyone? You should reserve it for yourselves. Never share it with strangers. Let your wife be a fountain of blessing for you. Rejoice in the wife of your youth. - Proverbs 5:15-18

Guys, you and I know that almost anyone can have sex. Just look around. It's everywhere and it's fighting for our attention and our minds. Casual sex has become such a prominent part of the culture and causes so many train wrecks in so many lives. You know the stories.

Does waiting until marriage sound old fashioned? And does waiting to have sex until after getting married really improve the quality of sex? According to Psychology Today, Professor Dean Busby of Brigham Young University had studied 2,035 married people ranging in age from 19 to 71, married from less than six months to more than 20 years.

Dr. Busby claimed that not only did the couples who waited until after marriage to have sex rate their sex life better, they reported that their marriages were more stable and satisfying. Their communication was also better than couples who had not waited.

I have been married for more than 15 years and I can tell you first hand that sex with my wife only gets better as the years go on. And when I say better, I mean we continue to communicate more freely, we laugh regularly and enjoy each other more intimately.

According to a survey published by the University of Chicago, only in cases where married couples are having sex a few times a year or not at all, do non-married adults rate higher than their married counterparts. By and large, married couples have sex more frequently than singles or cohabiting adults. Additionally, the survey suggest that sex is better among religious or spiritual couples. Can I get an amen?

Let's also teach our children that sex is a powerful force. Teach them that it's physically amazing, and once they start, it could be hard to stop. Teach them that sex is often confused with love, because having sex gives the false sense of intimacy.

When we have sex, we release the "bonding hormone" oxytocin, which makes us feel closer to that person. I want my boys to know that this is part of God's beautiful design he intended for us to enjoy only once we are married.

When we look at the words of Jesus in Matthew 19:5 we read, "For this reason, a man will leave his father and mother and be joined to his wife, and the two will become one flesh."

To the world, the point of sex is pleasure, release and orgasm. What other point would anyone need? Sex results in pleasure. I want pleasure, so I have sex. I want more pleasure; I have more sex. This is not the story I want my children to live out. I want them to know why it is essential to view sex as a good thing and I want them to see it as a gift that is best experienced and enjoyed for the first time on their wedding night.

Guys, you and I are co-writing the story for our children. If we are striving to model and disciple them with a biblical worldview, it will include boundaries that can lead them to sexual freedom.

I love Tim Keller's thoughts on why true freedom involves having some constraints. In his book, *Every Good Endeavor*, he says:

"Modern people like to see freedom as the complete absence of any constraints. But think of a fish. Because a fish absorbs oxygen from water, not air, it is free only if it is restricted to water. If a fish is 'freed' from the river and put on the grass to explore, its freedom to move and soon even to live is destroyed. The fish is not more free, but less free, if it cannot honor the reality of its nature. The same is true with airplanes and birds. If they violate the laws of aerodynamics, they will crash into the ground. But if they follow them, they will ascend and soar. The same is true in many areas of life: Freedom is not so much the absence of restrictions as finding the right ones, those that fit with the realities of our own nature and those of the world."

Freedom is not so much the absence of restrictions as finding the right ones, those that fit with the realities of our own nature and those of the world.

You would probably agree that without boundaries, guardrails and rules in general, our every day life would be in shambles. This includes the freedom that is found when we follow the design and purpose of sex within marriage. So if you agree, then share it with your children so that they have a chance to experience freedom from many of the heartaches that are often associated with premarital sex.

I'm not suggesting that you share about your personal sex life. On the contrary, please don't. Just don't treat sex as taboo. Begin teaching your boys that sex is a good thing that God has designed, and it is to be reserved exclusively for a man and woman within marriage to enjoy.

Take Aways:

1. Only a married man and woman should have sex.
2. Waiting until marriage will save a lot of heartache.
3. Sex is an extraordinary gift of God, that is best experienced when reserved for marriage.
4. The best approach is simple words, honest answers and easy analogies that children can understand for the stage they are in.

6

Sex Talk With Friends

In the same way, let your light shine before others, that they may see your good deeds and glorify your Father in heaven. - Matthew 5:16

My children know that my wife and I are the first point of contact and the safest place for conversations about sex. I use the word "safest" because they now know about the many misconceptions and possible dangers associated with this topic. There is no question that the sex topic will arise even among those who are young.

My sons know that when the topic of sex comes up, they don't need to be nervous, insecure or embarrassed. My sons know to direct the conversation to privacy and truth.

It is really important that we give them a vocabulary and a confident one at that. I coach them to say things like, "Dude, talking about sex is fine but it needs to be with your parents, not around us." Or even, "Hey man, let's keep our conversation honorable, it doesn't help anyone to joke about things like that."

My sons know that if they come to me at any time day or night to discuss sex that I'm a safe place and they won't be in any trouble whatsoever.

Let's chat for moment. Do you struggle with lust, pornography or other brokenness in this area? Recent studies show that 83% of men admit to struggling and I think nearly 17% aren't being truthful. Part of being able to lead our sons is knowing and admitting our own sin, struggles and pain. Even in our brokenness, we are not released from the responsibility to father our children in this area.

Part of my healing process has also been in finding trusted friends to walk along side me while I unpack my crazy and broken story. I share with and confess things to them so that light can transform the darkness in me and it's amazing how this process helps me become better at shining light in my sons unfolding stories. We need to be careful what we share with our sons about our past but they need to know that we are human and struggle as well. What we share needs to be a blessing to them and not a burden.

Confession isn't for forgiveness...it is for healing.

One of the most amazing revelations in my life is that of confession. Confession isn't for forgiveness…it is for healing. God doesn't need anything from you but He calls you to confess so that you will be healed in those places you think are too dark for anyone to love. If you do not have someone in your life to speak with about your struggles, I encourage you to pray that God would bring someone into your life that you can share with and begin your healing process.

Take Aways:

1. Build trust with your children so they know it is safe to talk to you about sex.
2. Give your children the vocabulary to be confident when sex talk comes up when you are not around.
3. If you haven't begun the healing process in your life, seek out men you can confide in.
4. Use simple words, honest answers and easy analogies.

7

Navigating Through A "Pornified" Culture

Stand firm then, with the belt of truth buckled around your waist, with the breastplate of righteousness in place. - Ephesians 6:14

If you are like me, then you probably want to help your child navigate through life without hitting the landmines of a hypersexualized, "pornified" culture.

Because most children have access to the internet, chances are they will come across sexualized content sooner than later. It is not "if" they will be exposed, it is a matter of "when". And this is one reason I believe in starting discussions with my children at a very early age.

For my children, I have given them a simple definition of what pornography is:

> *"Pornography is pictures or videos of people who have little or no clothing."*

When I was setting up restrictions on one of my boys' gaming systems, I used the opportunity to tell my oldest children, who were eight and eleven at the time, that I was doing this to help protect them from seeing images of naked people pop up on the screen.

> **It is not "if" they will be exposed, it is a matter of "when".**

We spoke about honoring women and how we should give girls the space and privacy they need—whether those girls are at the pool, at the beach, at the store, at the ballfields, or on TV and the internet.

We have an agreement together, to turn our eyes from any image of a girl without much clothes on. If we are walking through the mall and pass a picture of models, we look into each other's eyes. If a woman on TV is in a bra or similarly immodest clothing, we catch each other's eyes. We don't look at pornography or naked people, because they need privacy, even if they don't know it.

I was encouraged a few months ago when I learned that someone had been talking to my oldest about sex and pornography. When we debriefed, I asked him how it made him feel to hear about it from someone else. He said it didn't bother him. When I asked him why, he said, "Because you and I already talk about that stuff."

We don't look at pornography or naked people, because they need privacy, even if they don't know it.

If we educate our sons on the darkness of pornography and only tell them to look away, we stop short of validating this God-given longing for beauty. William Blake nailed it on the head when he said:

> "The naked woman's body is a portion of eternity too great for the eye of man."

This longing and attraction does not to be smothered or viewed as shameful. It needs to be validated, honored and shepherded over and over for many years.

Is there more than meets the eye when it comes to our deep desire for beauty? Is it possible that this ever increasing thirst is a glory and not a curse?

We have seen time and time again, through the ages, that men will risk their fortunes, reputations, businesses and their entire "kingdom" for what seems to be only a moment of pleasure. There is so much more to unpack here but on a basic level we have two choices: Are we consumers or are we living in our true nature as lovers and protectors?

> "The great divide lies between men as lovers and men as consumers. Does he seek her out, long for her, because really he yearns for her to meet some need in his life—a need for validation, or mercy, or simply sexual gratification? That man is a Consumer, as my friend Craig calls him. The lover, on the other hand, wants to fight for her—he wants to protect her, make her life better, wants to fill her heart in every way he can." - John Eldridge - Fathered By God

As I model this strength for my sons, my prayer is that they will see my desire is not to conquer beauty but to behold it. My goal in my marriage is to lay down my life and desires so that my wife will become more free to be all that God has made her to be.

As part of your ongoing conversations, begin to teach your boys that lust comes into play when we go from noticing a girl to wondering what she looks like naked or thinking about her sexually. Lust is desire gone mad and there are plenty of ways we take the good gifts of God and misuse them. Whether it's food, drink, work, exercise, you name it, we can mess it up. And you know as well as I do, that when it comes to the battle in our minds, our desires can go mad in a hurry.

When he sees pretty girls, on the internet particularly, he can become so curious that he might start looking at them without clothes on. And sometimes it can be hard to stop because often our brains don't know how to. Don't be afraid to talk to your son about this.

Many children will feel a variety of emotions when they are first exposed to pornography. Some may feel a sense of excitement. Some may be curious and continue seeking it out. Some will feel deep guilt and embarrassment. Others will feel a sense of excitement and shame mixed together.

I am hopeful that when my children are exposed to pornography, that they will be comfortable in addressing it with me. You can have the same confidence with your children as you begin having age-appropriate conversations.

Take Aways:

1. Plan on him being curious about girls and plan on it being sooner than you expect.
2. Plan to talk to him about sex and attraction regularly. See it as an ongoing conversation. Not a one-time talk.
3. Plan to let him know that the attraction he feels isn't a bad thing. Teach him that God designed attraction, intimacy, and sex as a beautiful gift for each of us to thoroughly enjoy inside the context of marriage.
4. Plan to make it clear that what happens in pornography today is not what girls want. It is not realistic. It is harmful to his mind and damaging to his relationships.
5. Plan on these types of conversation getting more natural for you as you lay the foundation for a healthy biblical view of sex.

8

When My Child Sees Pornography

Have I not commanded you? Be strong and courageous. Do not be frightened, and do not be dismayed, for the Lord your God is with you wherever you go.
-Joshua 1:9

For parents, it can be heartbreaking and confusing when you learn that your child has inadvertently been exposed to pornography or is viewing it regularly. You may even feel some guilt, anger, or embarrassment and those feelings would be reasonable. If that is the case for you, here are three tips for you in your moment of crisis:

- *Remain calm.* Breathe deep and take the necessary time to process what is happening and to get to an emotional level so you can respond to your child calmly. Why? Because your negative emotions can cause your child to feel a lot of shame and shame can often cause him to go into isolation and push him further into secrecy. Do you want to disarm him? Try getting on his level or below, look him in the eyes and smile at him.
- *Remember that you are on the same team.* Rather than using "YOU" and "I," try using "WE" and "US" to help convey that you are in this together and on the same team. Reassure him that you are not angry, but that you want to help him figure this out. Remind him that your relationship with him is very important and that you love him.
- *Create boundaries instead of delivering punishment.* If this is the first time your child has been exposed to pornography and it is followed by punishment, in their minds they will associate pornography struggles with being in trouble. Here is what they are thinking: *I'm in trouble, and my parents want to punish me. If I can't stop looking at pornography, I need to make sure I don't ever get caught again.*

If your boys don't have an issue with pornography or have not been exposed to it yet, that's wonderful—but remain diligent, because temptations are everywhere your kids look. This five-step family conversation plan is a practical approach to take with your children so you can have a conversation about pornography before they are exposed to it or as soon as you can after they view it. Tell them something like these statements:

1. "When you see pornography, turn off your device right away or get away immediately."
2. "When you see pornography, you can tell me about it without fear of being punished."
3. "If you accidentally see pornography, tell me so that we can create a plan to prevent it from happening again."
4. "If it was not accidental that you viewed pornography, let's talk through what is going on and how we can protect our hearts and minds from it."
5. "It is important that you understand that curiosity is normal and that a desire for knowledge of sexual things is healthy. It is equally important to know that pornography is not sex education, and what is seen in pornography is harmful to you."

What do you tell your boys if their friends are looking at pornography? We have made a plan when it comes to pressures that come from peers. I try to model proper responses and I encourage them to stand up for what they believe is right. Most kids are followers, and they usually gravitate toward a strong leader when they find one. I want to teach my children to lead well.

We have a "code word" that my boys can either text or say during a call or conversation when they want to let me know they are in a situation they want to get out of. Come up with your own code word. It can be as simple as "Hey dad, remember that double play" or "Dad, I think I have a stomach bug". Find what works for your family, and equip your children with the tools to get out of an unsafe situation.

One of the most important things you can do is have a continued conversation when it comes to sex. Don't try and unload all the details about reproduction, sex and pornography in one talk. That approach will either cause you to wait until they have already heard about sex from someone else or it will give them so much info that they don't know how to process it. The idea is to start the conversation and then continue it in the years to come. Much like we would with sports, faith or work.

And don't forget to use simple words, honest answers and easy analogies.

After you begin having the conversations, they will become less awkward. Then you can start adjusting your "chats" to fit your child's needs and maturity level.

And don't forget to use simple words, honest answers and easy analogies.

One of my favorite scriptures is Psalms 127:3-4 "Children are a heritage from the Lord, offspring a reward from him. Like arrows in the hands of a warrior are children born in one's youth." Our children are in our home, under our care and in the proximity of our influence to be intentionally pointed, launched and sent into the world to make an impact for the kingdom of God. It's not always easy to intentionally parent, but it's always worth it. And when we mess it up, let's be reminded that perfection is not the goal and it's not obtainable. Even so, by God's grace, let's continue to press on and raise boys to be men who will seek the Lord, protect the vulnerable and fight for the hearts of women. Thanks for joining me.

About The Author

Eric Poulin has been married to his beautiful wife Anna for 15 years and together they have four boys. As a family, they enjoy boating, sports, cooking and CrossFit.

A few years ago, Eric began learning about the commercial sex trade. He started learning about how young girls were being bought and sold for sex and he knew he had to do something about it.

Since then, Eric has lobbied Congress to pass laws that help protect sex trafficking victims. He has renovated a rescue home in Nashville for young girls who have been saved from sex trafficking. In 2016 Eric traveled to Thailand where he witnessed firsthand the commercial sex trade in Bangkok where men from all over the world were renting girls for sex.

Admittedly, he doesn't have it all together. He has struggled with lust and pornography himself, but he has also found redemption and is walking in freedom.

Eric has the idea that if he trains his four boys to reject pornography and teach them to honor, respect and protect girls, then the likelihood that they will grow up and purchase sex or participate in other forms of sexual exploitation will be significantly reduced.

He is also passionate about sharing with other fathers what he is learning and what is working for his family.

He believes that when like-minded men rally together, they can make an impact that will change the trajectory of the pornography, prostitution and sex trafficking business. Eric's vision is to see the demand for sex trafficking reduced and to see girls and women freed from it. This is the same vision which has led him to create *Forge and Foundry*, a community of fathers who train boys to be men of honor, wisdom and courage.

To inquire about Eric's speaking availability and scheduling, visit him at www.ericbpoulin.com

Connect With Eric

Instagram: @ericbpoulin
Facebook: @ericbpoulin

Connect with Forge and Foundry

Facebook: @forgeandfoundry.org
Web: forgeandfoundry.org

Made in the USA
Las Vegas, NV
05 June 2026

48141687R00036